September 2018
This book was donated by the
Oklahoma Hall of Fame
in Honor of Inductee
Justice Steven W. Taylor

EIGHT SEASONS OF THE HEREFORDS

RED DIRT BASEBALL IN ADA

Eight Seasons of the
HEREFORDS
Red Dirt Baseball in Ada

by PETER G. PIERCE

ISBN: 978-1-938923-01-2

Library of Congress Control Number: 2013930363

Oklahoma Heritage Association
1400 Classen Drive
Oklahoma City, Oklahoma 73106
405.235.4458
www.oklahomaheritage.com

 OKLAHOMA HERITAGE | Association

CONTENTS

INTRODUCTION

Eight Seasons of the Hereford—Red Dirt Baseball in Ada began as a chapter in a book in the Red Dirt Baseball Series about teams in the Chickasaw Nation. Near the completion of the first draft of that volume it was apparent that with all the materials provided by former players, owners, and their relatives there was enough to merit a separate book.

During the writing of *Baseball in the Cross Timbers: The Story of the Sooner State League*, Bill Thrash, long time executive with the Oklahoma Educational Television Authority whose father was a director of the Ada franchise in 1952 and 1953, provided photos and some recollections. After its publication, he gave me copies of a 1952 program and a number of articles and photos from the scrap book he kept between 1952 and 1954. Also during 2008, Joanna and Fern Smathers of Baton Rouge, Lousiana, graciously invited me to their home where they shared their memories of Ada and opened their scrapbooks. Additionally, they introduced me to their neighbor Bobby Tuminello who threw for the 1949 and 1950 McAlester Rockets and roomed with Hall of Famer Whitey Herzog.

Bob LaCross of San Diego had purchased the *Cross Timbers* book and kindly put me in contact with Bob King, West Coast scout for the Houston Astros, who was an alumnus of the 1948 and 1949 Herefords. He allowed me to scan his scrapbook and gave an interview. Van Yount, son of the late 1948 pitcher Bob Yount contacted me, provided photos and put me in touch with the 1948 catcher, Charles Hopkins of Columbia, Illinois who gave a long interview and shared his records not only from

his time at Ada but in the Texas League with San Antonio. Ann Milligan, daughter of 1949 and 1950 slugger Bill Milligan, was also in contact after reading *Baseball in the Cross Timbers*. She too provided photos.

While the base research for this book was done for *Baseball in the Cross Timbers*, the text is greatly expanded and contains much new information and many new photos published for the first time. There were no photos of Hereford Park, the rodeo arena *cum* ball park with the all-dirt field, in *Baseball in the Cross Timbers*. In Chapter Two there are seven. The stories of individuals are expanded and new ones written. Ada had a short but rich history in Organized Baseball. Only a handful of prospects for the St. Louis Browns and Baltimore Orioles who toiled there ever played in the Major Leagues but the hundreds of players who donned Hereford flannels left a legacy. It is my pleasure to tell their story.

—Peter G. Pierce

CHAPTER ONE

EIGHT SEASONS OF THE HEREFORDS

SEASON	ATTENDANCE	RECORD	FINISH	AFFILIATION	PLAYOFF FIRST ROUND	PLAYOFF FINALS
1947	41,872	86-51	2nd	St. Louis (AL)	Lost to McAlester 2-3	
1948	27,050	63-76	5th	St. Louis		
1949	33,525	69-70	4th	St. Louis	Lost to Pauls Valley 2-3	
1950	31,981	96-41	1st	St. Louis	Lost to Ardmore 2-3	
1951	12,779	54-86	5th	St. Louis		
1952	38,387	57-82	7th	St. Louis		
1953	36,128	84-54	3rd	St. Louis	Beat Shawnee 3-1	Lost to McAlester 1-4
1954	28,482	64-76	6th	Baltimore		

The St. Louis Browns between 1947 and 1953 had the lowest attendance in the American League each year, frequently hundreds of thousands less than their Sportsmen's Park tenant, the National League Cardinals. During this period they finished sixth once, seventh three times, and last the other four seasons, twice losing one hundred or more games. The only thing that improved when the Brownies became the Baltimore Orioles in 1954 was attendance; they still lost one hundred games. During these years, the Browns had an established minor league system, many scouts, and regularly a stable full of rookies and limited service players with potential. Unfortunately, few of those prospects were sent to Ada, the bottom rung of the organization's ladder. Bill Upton, who was released after three weeks and spent most of the 1948 season at Ardmore, was the first Hereford ever to suit up inside a Major League clubhouse and only then that of the Philadelphia Athletics as they were on their way out of town. Charlie Rabe (page 20) also appeared briefly for the Reds.

It was not until after the Ada franchise moved to Paris that the better players began to pass through. The Ada club, which had a full working agreement, was allowed to sign its own players and often did. Only the 1947 club with record attendance turned a small profit. The 1950 pennant winner only broke even. In every other season, the team lost between $5,000 and $14,000.

1947

Veteran baseball man Ucal "Uke" Clanton and civic booster Dr. Albert R. Sugg formed the Ada Baseball Club, Inc. on March 10, 1947, six months after the initial meeting in McAlester where the Sooner State League was formed. The company was capitalized with $10,000. Sugg, a prominent physician, and Clanton, an independent insurance agent, were the principal owners. Harrell Allen served as secretary-treasurer. Edwin Free, business manager, handled the financial and operating matters until midway through the 1947 season when George Morrison took over the front office. Clanton, who had appeared in one game for the 1922 Cleveland Indians, guided the team on the field. The Herefords' trainer was Ms. Gussie Pfeifer, Dr. Sugg's nurse. An office was set up at 106 ½ E. Main Street. The highest attendance in Ada's eight-

Bill Upton (1929-1987) with the 1948 Ardmore Indians following his release from Ada. He threw five innings without a decision for the last edition of the Philadelphia A's. He posted a 70-49 record in eight minor league seasons mainly in AAA and AA. He taught several Los Angeles Dodgers pitchers how to throw a fork ball.

Ada, ninety miles southeast of Oklahoma City, with a population of 15,000, was the center of "Hereford Heaven" where a three-day auction of prize cattle was held each January. The city boasted two large hotels, the Aldridge and Juliana, and three movie houses. Below: The team's namesake.

ABOVE: A sixteen-year-old rookie in 1945, Ray Kolafa (1929-2007) spent four seasons as an infielder in first the Cardinals' then the Browns' organizations. He is shown here in 1946 with the Carthage (MO) Cardinals of the K-O-M League. He hit .253 in 136 games for the 1947 Herefords.

Otto Utt (1906-1966) was the son of a cowboy and worked in the steel mills of Pueblo, Colorado until he curtailed a minor league career to catch for the semi-pro champion Halliburton Oil Cementers during the 1930s. Obstinate, parsimonious, and an advocate of small ball, Utt declined the New York Giants' offer of a working agreement in 1947. Instead, his Sooner State League Cementers finished last in the league and last in Organized Baseball in attendance with a scant 8,220 paying fans.

Paul Richardville (1923-1997) broke into Organized Baseball in 1946 finishing in Class C with the Browns' Aberdeen, S.D. club. He led the 1947 Herefords in hitting with a .304 average and the Sooner State League with eleven homers and 111 RBIs. For 1948 he was traded into the New York Giants' organization for two seasons. He finished his professional career with Chickasha in 1950. He died in Ada.

year professional history was achieved in its initial season when 41,872 went through the turnstiles at the 12,000-seat Hereford Park.

Since Chattanooga Lookouts owner Joe Engel, the "Barnum of the Bushes," began contests involving fans, players, and owners during the Depression, minor league clubs had put on entertaining but silly diversions. Early in the season, the Ada fans were treated to a foot race to first base between Dr. Sugg and owner-manager Otto Utt of the visiting Duncan Cementers. With Utt having to get past a man standing in the baseline and Dr. Sugg running backward, Utt won when Dr. Sugg fell and shattered his elbow. Dr. Sugg's injury notwithstanding, 1947 would be the Herefords' best season.

Despite the contestants committing eleven errors, the Herefords got off to the right start on April 29, 1947, when they beat Ardmore fourteen to thirteen on Ray Kolafa's pinch hit double in the bottom of the ninth. Ardmore catcher Dick Patterson earned the distinction of being the first player in

League history to be ejected from a game when he was tossed in the bottom of the second inning. After three weeks of play, outfielder Paul Richardville was hitting .400 and veteran hurler Joe Isaacs was leading the League with a 3-0 record. Ada was in second place behind pacesetter Lawton and would remain there the rest of the season. On June 24, Charlie Mize tossed the League's first ever no-hitter, a seven-inning affair, zeroing out McAlester one nil.

The mid-season All-Star team that played pacesetter Lawton included six Herefords: manager Ucal Clanton, Paul Deters, Richardville, Bob Koepka, Jack Wilson and Forest Smith; only Richardville and Smith would be named to the post-season team. At mid-season, except for pitchers and catchers, only two Herefords were playing at the same position where they had begun the season.

Henry Kane went on a hitting tear the last two weeks of the season and received cash from the fans through the fence nearly equal to his salary. Previously in the August 1 game against Lawton

The Ada Herefords regularly placed advertisements for games in the local newspaper. This one is from 1947 about a series with archrival McAlester.

The Sooner State League paid $14.95 per dozen for the official league ball manufactured by Worth. Every player from the years before 1950 confirmed that it was a "dead" ball. When the Worth ball failed to come within two percent of Major League specifications, the league let its contract to Rawlings. Home run production went from 399 in 1949 to 710 in 1950 with the change of balls.

at Hereford Park, he was cheated out of a home run by an umpire's call. He hit a shot to center but neither the umpires nor most players from either dugout could find the ball. Finally, a boy scrambled atop the bull chutes discovering a ball. Kane was awarded a double.

In hitting, Richardville led the League with eleven home runs and 111 RBIs. Forest "Woody" Smith was tops with twenty-three wins and a 2.00 ERA. Bill Donaghey sent 244 batters to the dugout with bat in hand. Averaging nightly attendance of 598, the club made a profit. In a game marred by nine Ada errors, the Herefords turned the first triple play in League history on August 25 against Duncan. Against fourth-place McAlester in the first round of the playoffs, Ada ended its season losing three of five to the Rockets who went on to take the League's first post-season championship over Ardmore.

1948

Uke Clanton was back at the helm in 1948 starting from scratch.

Like the 1947 team, fifteen players and equipment traveled in two station wagons, one driven by Clanton and the other by one of the players. A combination of Browns' farmhands and Clanton's local free agents could only muster sixty-three wins against seventy-six losses for fifth place in 1948. Without 1947's league-leading pitching, the fans stayed away with only 27,050 paying customers cheering "The Cat" Clanton's last team.

Managers Uke Clanton and Hugh Willingham of Seminole review their charges before a game at Ada.

BONUS PAY

BELOW: In Flatbush, a player could win a new suit by hitting the Abe Stark sign under the Ebbets Field scoreboard.

ABOVE: There were similar signs in virtually every minor league ballpark with the one in Durham, N.C. the most famous.

In the low minors, every league had a monthly salary cap. Because of that, only a few teams gave bonuses for outstanding plays. According to 1948 catcher Charles Hopkins, stolen bases, strike outs, and catching an opposing runner stealing were each worth 50¢.

To get around the Sooner State League salary cap, Opie Turner, wife of oil millionaire Waco Turner, paid bonuses to Ardmore Cardinals players in 1953-1954 that often equaled a player's monthly salary. More frequently, the fans were the benefactors. For a home run or game winning play, the hat would be passed with the star receiving up-wards of $20 in change. With the award, that lucky player would take some teammates to dinner.

The 1948 Herefords had an average age of 20.5 years. Twenty-seven prospects wore Herefords flannels that season. Top L-R: Earl Bossenberry, Charles Hopkins, Dennis Rackley, Wayne Ingram, Frank Hensley, Ucal Clanton, Arnold Spence, Art Punkyo, and Mel Knopp. Lower L-R: Bob Yount, Mack Hyde, Harry Vice, Everett Neal (?), Virl Loman, James Howard, and Bobby King.

Orville Makintubee (1925-2005), who had been an All-State football player at Ada High School, was in his sophomore professional season following a record of seven wins against four losses for his hometown Herefords in 1947.

Tom Kruta (1926-1997) was a prize prospect in the Cleveland system.

Bob Yount's first and only home run ball.

The season began with Ada's Orville Makintubee squaring off against Ardmore's rookie phenom, Tom Kruta of Oklahoma City, at the Indians' Tribe Park. Makintubee scattered eleven hits but five Ardmore errors allowed eight Ada runs for a four-run victory. Ardmore returned the favor the following evening jumping on Charlie Mize for twelve hits that, combined with Mel Knopp's four errors, allowed fourteen Indians' runs while the Herefords plated but a solo score; Mize quit baseball after that. The Adans dropped the next five contests before Charles Hopkins' first round tripper of the season at the Duncan Bowl gave Bob Yount his first win.

The excitement came with the Herefords on defense as they turned a pair of triple plays. The first occurred on May 30 in a seven to three win at Ardmore. The Ardmore batter lined deep to left fielder Arnold Spence who threw a strike to catcher

Harry Vice (1930-) was remembered by his 1948 Hereford teammates as a fine pitcher. A record of fifteen wins in twenty-six decisions with a 3.85 ERA was his best of five professional seasons spent in Louisiana and Gulf Coast Texas.

Bob Stautzenbach (1925-2011) roamed the outfields in Ada and Chickasha for two seasons hitting .220. He joined Orville Makintubee and Art Punkyo as Ada alumni on the 1948 Chiefs.

Hopkins, doubling up the runner coming from third. Hopkins then threw out the Ardmore runner on second base with a perfect peg to shortstop Dennis Rackley who applied the tag. The other was performed before the home fans on June 21 in a four to two loss to McAlester. With the bases loaded with Rockets, first baseman Earl Bossenberry fielded a grounder then threw to the plate for the force out. Catcher Hopkins fired the ball to Bobby King who was covering first to retire the batter. King then threw back to Hopkins to nail the McAlester runner trying to score.

It was not a case of sabotage when the Herefords treated the visiting Chickasha Chiefs to a steak feed on July 1 that put 1947 Hereford Bob Stautzenbach in the hospital with food poisoning. Orville Makintubee gained some revenge against his former teammates that evening as he tamped down the Herefords for his seventh win since being released.

Harry Vice's nine inning no-hitter against Lawton on July 13 was emblematic of the 1948 season. Three errors in the fifth inning, including one by Vice himself handling Lawton pitcher Bob Gidding's bunt, allowed an unearned Giants' run to score giving them the win 1-0. There were few other high points.

Immediately before the June 21 game, Ada shortstop Dennis Rackley—a converted softball pitcher and team clown—of Chandler, Oklahoma, married lovely Betty Mattheyer at home plate.

The 1948 Herefords even found a way to lose a doubleheader despite the fact that they outscored their opponent in each game. Chickasha protested an August 22 game, which the Chiefs won, because Ada had signed 1947 regular, Ray Kolafa, after the August 17 deadline. As a result, the Herefords forfeited an August 20 sweep of a doubleheader from Pauls Valley. The Ada nine limped to a 63-76 fifth-place finish. The cussing that umpire Tex Burnett directed to Rackley, Vice, Seminole manager Hugh Willingham, and the fans on September 2, as Ada lost to the Oilers sixteen to twelve, just added insult to the injury of a second division season.

The 1948 edition led the League with 958 runs scored and seventy-one home runs, but its batters also made 848 strike outs and left 1,286 on base. With two triple plays and the top figures in put outs and assists it is initially surprising that the club was only in the middle of the pack in fielding but 368

Bobby King played the keystone for the Herefords in 1948 and 1949. Today he is the West Coast scout for the Houston Astros. The wooden, free-standing "dugout" is behind him.

Frank Hensley (1927-) led the Herefords with fifteen home runs, 100 runs batted in, and a .440 slugging percentage. He reached Class B in 1954.

Mack Hyde (1926-1994) was promoted to his hometown Muskogee Reds of the Western Association midway through the 1948 season.

Mr. and Mrs. Dennis Rackley

Best man Bob Yount (1919-2011) was assigned to the Kitty League late in the season where he finished his playing career in 1950. He returned to his home of Leadwood, Missouri where he retired from St. Joe Lead in 1984 and later ran The Bank of the Leadbelt until retiring in 1991.

Catcher Charles Hopkins (1926-) hit .269 in 129 games behind the plate. He spent his entire career in the Browns' organization including 1952-1954 as the regular catcher for the San Antonio Missions of the Texas League. He managed the 1955 Seminole Oilers in the Sooner State League.

Dennis Rackley (1926-2003) skipped 1949 and was a regular for the independent Seminole Oilers in 1950 and early 1951. He worked for the Midland Oil Refinery in Cushing, Oklahoma for a number of years. His marriage lasted fifty-five years.

Virl Loman (1910- 1993) pitched mainly home games because his day job was running his Texaco station at Main and Mississippi in Ada. According to Bobby King, he had a vicious knuckle curve. He pitched both ends of a double header for the 1948 Herefords. He tossed for Seminole in 1950 before returning to the Herefords in 1952 as interim manager. He died in Moreno Valley, California.

errors explains the .936 fielding percentage; forty-six passed balls exacerbated the glove problem. Pitching was the weak spot. Virl Loman's 3.72 ERA was the team's best. No player led the League in any category, nor were any selected for inclusion on the All-Star team.

While 1948 began with money in the bank, the attendance drop of nearly 15,000, which translated to an operating loss of approximately $9,750, nearly wiped out both the initial paid-in capital plus the club's surplus profit from 1947. For Sugg, the Herefords had ceased to be a hobby and became work. For Clanton, the team could not afford the luxury of a non-playing manager. It was time to sell.

From a player's standpoint, however, things were not so bad. Ada fans were among the League's most enthusiastic and generous when it came to the low minor league custom of passing cash through the fences and backstops directly to players who had outstanding plays or hit home runs. Ada did

Hugh Willingham (1906-1988) played for the Phillies and White Sox before taking over the Seminole Oilers in 1947. He managed Ardmore briefly in 1952 and was business manager when baseball returned to Seminole in 1954.

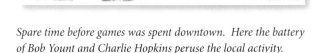

Spare time before games was spent downtown. Here the battery of Bob Yount and Charlie Hopkins peruse the local activity.

not need an appreciation night. Every game was potentially an appreciation event. On September 5, 1948, the day after the season ended, Robert W. Cason, Jr., a local Ford dealer and American Legion ball sponsor, announced that he was buying Sugg's and Clanton's stock to become controlling shareholder of Ada Baseball Club, Inc. He kept George Morrison, also a shareholder, in the front office. E.W. Kemp, who had been a minority shareholder with Sugg and Clanton, retained his investment.

1949

Under new ownership and new field leadership in the form of Bill Krueger, the expectations for 1949 were upbeat. Sophomore Earl Bossenberry, sophomore Bill King, and rubber-armed reliever and semi-pro veteran Virl Loman returned from 1948.

Two future stars of the champion 1950 Hereford team would be picked up on the bounce from the White Sox's Seminole club. Bill Milligan, who had been a regular in fifty-four Oiler games, and rookie Steve Molinari, who had appeared in nine contests in Seminole flannels, would light up League pitching in 1950 like a pinball machine. But neither Milligan nor Molinari had a particularly sterling season in 1949. While setting a League record with McAlester for playing 143 games in a 140-game season, Herefords carried their bats back to the dugout 987 times, more frequently than any other club, and the team batting average was last at .230. The .935 fielding average was in the middle of the Sooner State League pack. Gardner, Grass and Loman all had respectable ERAs under 3.50 but the batters just did not score enough runs.

A month into the season, no Hereford was hitting over .285. Rookie outfielder Fred Boiko set the all-time Sooner State League record for most hits in an inning: a home run and two singles in a twenty-four to three romp over Lawton. The seventeen

Bill Krueger-MGR   Jack Ray-SS   Ted Gardner LHP   Les Williams OF   Vir Louran RHP   Bill Milligan OF

Earl Bossenberry 1B   Ricky   Don   Fred Boyko (OF)   Len Zilberg (C)   Bobby King 2B

Cason's 1949 Hereford's sported new uniforms and under Bill Krueger's leadership won a playoff berth.

Earl Bossenberry (1928 -) broke in with Mayfield in the Kitty League in 1948 before the Browns sent him to their Ada club. He was released following a .274 1949 season with the Herefords then, moving up to the class C Evangeline League, hit .330 and .306 for New Iberia. He finished his professional career in 1952 at age twenty-four with Midland of the Longhorn League batting .309. He graduated from Eastern Michigan University lettering in basketball in 1953 and 1954. He enjoyed a successful career in financial management and heads a private foundation in Michigan.

Ada runs scored in the seventh inning of that game also set a record. Bill Milligan's twenty-third home run in the season finale on September 4 gave Ada a win over Ardmore and put him in a tie with future New York Giants shortstop Daryl Spencer of Pauls Valley for the most four baggers in a season, a record that would stand until July 10 of the next season. In a close semi-final series, the first-place Pauls Valley Raiders sent the Adans to their off-season homes three games to two.

1950

The next year, also under Krueger, Cason accompanied the Herefords to the Browns' minor league spring training camp in Pine Bluff, Arkansas. They returned with the best Ada team that ever took the field, winning a franchise record ninety-six games. The 1950 Herefords had strong hitting and solid pitching to take the regular season pennant before 31,981 but lost the championship to McAlester in the playoffs. To shore up the franchise financially, several investors signed "limited liability

BELOW: 1949 Pitching staff L-R: Bob Tobey, Frank Grass, John Schwartz, Ted Gardner, Hal Wilfong, and Ben Burch.

1949 Infield L-R: shortstop Henry Pengel,third baseman Jack Ray, second baseman Bobby King, and first baseman Earl Bossenberry.

BELOW: 1949 Outfielders L-R: Fred Boiko, Les Williams, Bill Milligan, and Steve Molinari.

1949 Catchers: left Bernie Odasz, and right Leonard Zeibig.

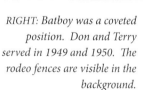

RIGHT: Batboy was a coveted position. Don and Terry served in 1949 and 1950. The rodeo fences are visible in the background.

notes" that could be advanced on by a lender at Cason's request to fund the ball club should operating revenues be insufficient. Fortunately for the signers, Cason announced that the Herefords would have a fair season if they drew above 500 for the last home stand. The team broke even in 1950 and no money was borrowed.

Bill Krueger, at age twenty-seven, assembled a club that led the League in most hitting catego-ries. With 188 home runs, including a number over Hereford Park's short right- and center-field fences, they surpassed the League record by eighty-four. With one thousand RBIs on the season and seven starters hitting over .310, the Herefords won ninety-six and lost only forty-one to finish five and one-half games ahead of second-place McAlester. The team batting average was .300. Fielding was middling: .931 with 354 errors. In June, coming off a sixteen-game winning streak with seventy team home runs and Milligan hitting .400, second sacker Ron Jackson at .425, and Molinari at .367, the Herefords attracted national attention in a story in *The Sporting News* on June 14, 1950, "Browns Blasting Farm Team Rocking Sooner Loop with Blasts."

It was not all beauty, however. Before the streak began, Ada and Pauls Valley combined on May 4 for one of the sloppiest examples ever of impersonating professional baseball teams. The two nines combined for fourteen balks that scored seven runs, eighteen walks, thirty hits, thirty-nine runs, five batters hit, two wild pitches, and ten errors. Somehow Ada managed to win by a football score of twenty-two to seventeen. Milligan ended the season with thirty-seven homers as Molinari set the all-time Sooner State League record with thirty-nine plus a

league best162 RBIs. Don Davenport added thirty-two round trippers, Fred Boiko twenty-four, and manager Krueger twenty-one.

The 1950 Herefords had sound pitching. Bill Donaghey, a twenty-two game winner in 1947, was back to lead the League in wins and percentage, twenty-six wins against five losses and .839. Workhorse Glass chipped in another twenty wins. In his only season in Organized Ball, Bill Starr lost only one in eleven decisions but had a huge 7.86 ERA. The playoff jinx continued, however. This year Ardmore sent Ada home early winning three of five. Five Adans made the All-Star team: Davenport at first, manager Krueger at third, Steve Molinari outfield, Bill Milligan utility, and Bill Donaghey on the mound.

The bottom line in the front office was not nearly as stunning as the team's performance on the field. As owner Cason explained in August, nightly paid attendance of six hundred was the breakeven point. At that time the club was $8,000 in the red and averaging only 334 paid admissions. Then fans responded but only enough to raise the average figure to 457. They showed their appreciation for the players on the last night of the season passing the hat to raise $1,126.03 to be divided among the seventeen players on the roster and disabled list.

There was a super fan that the team recognized in 1950. Mrs. Ruby Emerich of Ada had watched every Ada game, home and road, from 1947 through 1950. For that she was recognized by the team with an autographed baseball. During the off-season, the Herefords made a contribution to community life. Barnstorming Stars led by the Yankees' Super Chief Allie Reynolds played an Ada team organized by McAlester manager and catcher Vern Hoscheit on October 15, 1950.

ABOVE: *1950 Ada Sluggers L-R: Bill Milligan, Steve Molinari, Fred Boiko, Bill Krueger.*

RIGHT: *Fred Grass (20-7 3.65) played both of his professional seasons at Ada.*

1951

At the height of the military draft for the Korean conflict, lower classification players became increasingly scarce. A pitcher who appeared briefly on the 1950 team after his release from Ponca City, John Lazar,was killed in action on September 7, 1951.

Stan Galle, a good teacher, left scouting to take over the short-handed Herefords. The 1951 season got off to an inauspicious start with McAlester routing the Herefords at home fourteen to one. The Herefords stumbled their way to only one win in the next six games. On May 12, Ada and McAlester pitchers served up thirty-four walks, a Sooner State League record, in the Rockets' twenty-four to eighteen triumph. Short on pitchers, Jim Harper went the distance against Ardmore on May 23, giving up twenty-one hits and allowing eleven walks in chalking up one of his nineteen losses by a twenty to nine tally. At June 14, the Adans were in the cellar, having won only thirteen of fifty-three outings. By the Fourth of July they had climbed to seventh place at twenty-four victories against fifty defeats only because Seminole had gone into a tail spin losing fourteen of sixteen games.

The Herefords ended McAlester star Dee Sanders' season string of seventy-five and one-third consecutive innings without a walk in the second inning of the nightcap on July 4 when Merle Barth was passed. Sanders went on to his thirteenth win eleven to two. On July 9, Ada matched the League record for most errors in a game with nine in losing to McAlester. Three weeks later, the club had won six of twenty-one to remain in seventh. On August 8, Detroit rookie Joe Carolan, sent down on July 19 by K-O-M member Pittsburg, Kansas, belted the team's only grand slam of 1951 against Seminole. Combining an August Herefords rally with Chickasha and Lawton fading lifted Ada to fifth place where they finished the season forty-six and

Corporal John Lazar

Dee Sanders (1921-2007) appeared briefly with the 1945 St. Louis Browns after starring with Dale Mitchell at the University of Oklahoma in 1941. He owned a business in McAlester and only pitched home games winning twenty-seven with a 1.67 ERA. 1951 was his last season before being elected Sheriff of Pittsburg County.

one-half games out of first. The April through July slump injured the Ada club's bottom line irreparably with an average attendance of 183, far below the six hundred needed to pay the bills.

Leading the League in batters striking out with 1,116, the 1951 Herefords managed a team batting average of only .248, sixth in the League. Playing 141 games at second base, Galle led the team in hitting at .317. Shortstop Jack Ray, a Pontotoc County player, was the only other Hereford to hit above .300. While leading the Sooner State League with 142 double plays, the fielding was not very good in other areas. The team fielding average was .930 with 388 errors or 2.75 per game. The catchers allowed fifty-four passed balls; Dick Sobeck had twenty-one in forty games but he redeemed himself in the outfield with a .977 percentage. Pitching was the weakest point. In 1,200 innings, Ada hurlers gave up 1,391 hits, 1,150 runs—only 843 of them earned—and 904 free passes. The staff committed twenty-three balks and unleashed eighty-one wild pitches. The combined ERA, not surprisingly, was worst in the League at 6.33.

The 1951 season was a disappointment both on the field and in the stands. The fifth-place club had the worst record in Herefords history. Having proved that they would not support a loser, the Ada team under the guidance of first-year manager Stan Galle played before only 12,779, just a few more than capacity of Hereford Park for one game. In the eleven years of the Sooner State League, only Duncan's hapless 1947 Cementers with 8,220 viewers had a worse gate.

Cason could not sell enough cars to support his baseball adventure and the other investors were unwilling to risk more money. When a group was being formed to purchase the assets of the Ada club in 1952, the Herefords' business manager, George Morrison, related to a meeting of potential investors that the cost of running a Sooner State League team would be in the $35,000 range including:

- Wages for the manager and players $16,000
- Salary for the business manager .... $ 1,800
- Road expenses .... $ 5,000
- League dues .... $ 2,250
- Uniforms .... $ 1,500
- Bats and balls .... $ 2,000
- Park maintenance .... $ 1,000
- Utilities .... $ 2,000
- Taxes and insurance .... $ 500
- Telephone, telegraph, office .... $ 1,000

He said that the club needed 60,000 paid attendance to break even. The revenues from other sources were simply too little to sustain the operation. The Browns paid $1,500 under the working agreement, concessions netted $2,500 for a season, program advertising brought in $1,400, all the box seats went for $1,800, while season ticket sales never totaled more than $500. This was typical of most Sooner State League teams.

1952

The franchise was sold to Ada Baseball Association, Inc. headed by oilman Lawrence Sanford, Jr. and auto dealer Guy Thrash. With an infusion of cash and enthusiasm, and nearly nightly promotions, the 1952 Herefords were looking for a turnaround. W.A. Delaney and Erwin Hovis served as vice president and secretary-treasurer, respectively, while Foster McSwain, George McRobert, Roy Lawler, and Luther Edge rounded out the board of directors. With initial capitalization of $25,000 and over one-hundred shareholders, the new ownership was optimistic.

Charlie Rabe (1932-) pitched ten seasons in the minor leagues in the Cincinnati organization amassing a record of 115 wins and 105 losses. He lost all four decisions for the Cincinnati Reds in 1957-1958.

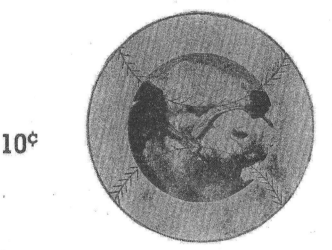

AUTO LOANS AND FINANCING

Save Money

SEE

The First National Bank

ADA, OKLAHOMA   PHONE 32

ADA HEREFORDS

10¢   10¢

1952

HELP THE HEREFORDS

by

PATRONIZING THE CONCESSION STAND
ALL MONEY GOES TO THE CLUB

Thanks
GENE LOWE, Mgr.

While most clubs in the low minors printed simple scorecards, under Sanford's ownership a full eight-page program was produced including the story of Ada Baseball Association, Inc., the new owner. The cover encourages fans to patronize the concessions stand operated by the club. It lost money in 1952. For 1953, concessions were outsourced to Lawrence Reynolds, shop teacher at Ada Junior High School.

"Ada Baseball Association, Inc."

Some time during January, 1952, the word leaked out that ADA was about to lose the Ada Baseball club, some three other cities were in the market for the Franchise.

About a half dozen Business and Professional men interested in baseball got to talking on the street corners. Something should be done, these few men got in touch with Bob Cason, Jr., owner of the Ada Baseball Club to find out the score. Then these same few men met in an office to discuss the possibilities of calling a public meeting of men and women interested in keeping the Club here in Ada. The meeting was a huge success.

At this meeting Guy H. Thrash was appointed General Chairman and he picked about a half dozen men to help him to try to organize a new Corporation to buy the assets and the Franchise of the Ada Base Ball Club from it's owner Bob Cason, Jr. Several meetings were held, and it was decided to issue stock in a new organization to be known as the ADA BASEBALL ASSOCIATION, INC.

Baseball fans were contacted and the plan met with the approval of most people contacted. More meetings were held, with progress being rather enthusiastic so another public meeting was called and the progress of the committee was presented. At this meeting the new organization was formed. The following were elected to the Board of Directors:

Lawrence E. Sanford, President
Roy J. Lollar, Vice-Pres.
Erwin T. Hovis, Sec'y.-Treas.
Guy H. Thrash, Member
Luther Edge, Member
Dr. O. H. Miller, Member
Geo. G. MacRoberts, Member

This seven-member board was elected to serve for a term of one year. With the assistance of a proper legal staff the corporation was formed.

Other meetings were held and the deal was completed with Mr. Cason with only about five weeks before the season was to open. These members of the newly elected Board had plenty to do with from two to three meetings a week and several hours spent in each one of them. Finally the season is about to open.

This Ass'n. belongs not to the Board of Directors but to the citizens of Ada and the surrounding cities, even as far as Oklahoma City. There are approximately 100 stockholders and others are invited to participate if they are interested. They may contact any member of the Board. This is a $25,000.00 corporation.

The members of the Board of Directors wish to take this opportunity to thank each and every one who has been so cooperative in this movement.

SCORING MADE EASY

Baseball Shorthand as Used by Baseball Writers Waich Will Render Every Game More Enjoyable to Baseball Enthusiasts. All Players are Numbered and All Plays Recorded by Symbols.

NUMBER PLAYERS AS FOLLOWS:

Pitcher ... 1	Second Baseman ... 4	Left Fielder ... 7
Catcher ... 2	Third Baseman ... 5	Center Fielder ... 8
First Baseman ... 3	Short Stop ... 6	Right Fielder ... 9

PLAYER POSITION

ADA HEREFORDS

	1	2	3	4	5	6	7	8	9	10	AB	R	1B	SH	PO	A	E

SUPPORT YOUR TEAM

See Schedule on Page 7 — And Plan Now to

Attend Every Home Game

Base Hit		Fielder's Choice	FC	Sacrifice Hit	H	Muffed Fly	
Two-base Hit		Hit by Pitcher	HP	Passed Ball	B	Wild Throw	
Three-base Hit		Wild Pitch	WP	Balk	BK	Force Out	X
Home Run		Stolen Base		S Struck Out	K		
Fumbled Grounder	A	Left on Bases	L	Base on Balls	BB		

SYMBOLS FOR PLAYS

An illustration will show the method of recording a play. In the upper left-hand corner opposite batter's name A—4 means batter reached first on fumble by second baseman. In the upper right-hand corner S means he stole second. In the lower right-hand corner B means he reached third on passed ball. In the lower left-hand corner 1—2 means he was thrown out to catcher at plate by shortstop.

PLAYER POSITION

VISITORS

	1	2	3	4	5	6	7	8	9	10	AB	R	1B	SH	P.O	A	E

62
AB
O.

ed and
rated by
ll Malloy

ADA HEREFORDS
1952 SCHEDULE

ADA AT HOME		ADA ABROAD	
April 17, 18	McAlester	April 19, 20	McAlester
April 23, 24	Lawton	April 21, 22	Sherman
April 25, 26	Shawnee	April 27, 28	Lawton
May 1, 2	Sherman	April 29, 30	Shawnee
May 3, 4	Ardmore	May 7, 8	Ardmore
May 5, 6	Chickasha	May 9, 10	Pauls Valley
May 11, 12	Pauls Valley	May 13, 14	Chickasha
May 15, 16	McAlester	May 17, 18	McAlester
May 21, 22	Lawton	May 19, 20	Sherman
May 23, 24	Shawnee	May 25, 26	Lawton
May 29, 30	Sherman	May 27, 28	Shawnee
May 31	Ardmore	June 4, 5	Ardmore
June 1	Ardmore	June 6, 7	Pauls Valley
June 2, 3	Chickasha	June 10, 11	Chickasha
June 8, 9	Pauls Valley	June 14, 15	McAlester
June 12, 13	McAlester	June 16, 17	Sherman
June 18, 19	Lawton	June 22, 23	Lawton
June 20, 21	Shawnee	June 24, 25	Chickasha
June 26, 27	Sherman	July 2, 3	Ardmore
June 28, 29	Ardmore	July 4, 5	McAlester
June 30	Chickasha	July 8, 9	Sherman
July 1	Chickasha	July 10, 11	Lawton
July 6, 7	McAlester	July 16, 17	Pauls Valley
July 12, 13	Shawnee	July 22, 23	Shawnee
July 14, 15	Lawton	July 24, 25	Chickasha
July 18, 19	Chickasha	July 30, 31	Ardmore
July 20, 21	Pauls Valley	August 1, 2	McAlester
July 26, 27	Sherman	August 3, 4	Sherman
July 28, 29	Ardmore	August 9, 10	Pauls Valley
August 5, 6	Shawnee	August 15, 16	Shawnee
August 7, 8	Lawton	August 17, 18	Chickasha
August 11, 12	Chickasha	August 23, 24	Ardmore
August 13, 14	Pauls Valley	August 27, 28	Chickasha
August 19, 20	Sherman	August 29, 30	Lawton
August 21, 22	Ardmore	September 2, 3	Pauls Valley
August 25, 26	Pauls Valley		
August 31	McAlester		
September 1	McAlester		

The Browns assigned thirty-year-old coach Bill Enos, who had managed the Browns' Pittsburg, Kansas K-O-M League team in 1951, to lead the 1952 Herefords. Over 2,200 fans showed up for the opening day win over McAlester and the Herefords responded by finishing the first week of the season tied for first place.

By the second week, they had dropped to third. A winning streak brought their record to fourteen and five and into second place, one-half game behind Pauls Valley. Charlie Rabe joined the team as a highly recruited rookie but lasted only three weeks before receiving his release because he was wild. A few days later, Lawton signed him and he proceeded to toss eighteen consecutive perfect innings for the little Reds.

After June 5, the Herefords collapsed losing nineteen of twenty-four games and falling to seventh. On July 13, the Herefords set a League record using seven pitchers in a ten-inning, nineteen to ten loss to Shawnee. The slump continued as the team won only twelve of forty-six contests from June 5 to July 17. On July 10, south central Oklahoma suffered monsoon-like rains. When the sun came out, the all-dirt field at Hereford Park was covered with several hundred gallons of gasoline and burned; even that did not dry the infield sufficiently for play.

There was friction between the management and Enos who was on the Herefords' payroll. By the beginning of August with the Herefords mired in seventh place, exacerbated by financial hemorrhaging, the simmering conflict between Sanford's and Enos' personalities spilled over. On August 5, with the Herefords still in seventh with forty-seven

1952 Ada Herefords. L-R: Top row: O'dell Hightower, Dick Sobeck, Don Dielman, Bob Barron, Neil Thode, Moose Arnone, Ron Slawski, and Jim England. Front row: Doc McCarn, James Cumbie, Mike Goffredo, Jack Nichols, Lou Medina, Boots Bowers, and interim manager Virl Loman. Hightower (1930-2006), a native Adan, got a tryout as a pitcher with the Herefords after graduating from Napier High School in Ada. He does not appear in any records of Organized Baseball but the records of the Sooner State League show him with three balks in fewer than 27 innings.

wins against sixty-two defeats, Enos, despite being well-liked by the players, was fired and returned to the front office in St. Louis as a scout and minor league instructor. At that point, Sanford, on behalf of ownership, made public the team's desperate condition: it was $8,000 in debt with only twelve home dates left.

The Herefords set a record with seven home runs against Chickasha on August 16, to impress new manager and part-time pitcher Virl Loman. Loman stayed until August 22, when he went back to pumping gas and nineteen-year old Jim England, who played for Enos in 1951, finished the season at the helm in seventh place, twenty-nine and one-half games behind McAlester. Batting .273 as a team, third best in the League, mediocre fielding and poor pitching doomed the 1952 Herefords from the outset. England set a League record with 612 at bats. He and Dick Sobeck hit .324 and .348, respectively. Only rookie pitcher Harry Byfuss with eight wins against five losses and a 4.63 ERA had a winning record; he was sold to the Senators' organization. The lowest ERA on the team was Charles Kreeger's 4.32. The other starters allowed far too many opponents to cross the plate: Neil Thode ERA 5.15, Endoro Arnone ERA 5.39, Fred Schak ERA 6.20, Joe McCormack ERA 6.40, and Jack Nichols, the leader with eighteen wild pitches, ERA 8.64.

While final attendance was up to 548 per date, considerably better than 1951's 183, 16,000 more than 1951, it still was not enough to pay the bills. Whether baseball would return in 1953 was problematic.

1953

The Herefords' board of directors faced three critical issues as preparations for the 1953 season began. The first was hiring a manager who could get along with Lawrence Sanford and was acceptable to the St. Louis Browns' minor league manage-ment. The second was whether to accept African-American players on assignment from the Browns. The third was how to promote ticket sales, the life blood of minor league franchises.

The dean of Sooner State League managers, Lou Brower, was lured away from the Giants' Pauls Valley farm club soon after the November 16, 1952 annual owners' meeting. Browns farm director, James McLaughlin, informed the Herefords that there were a number of outstanding African-American prospects available. The Sooner State League was not segregated as Arthur Willingham had broken the color line the previous season at Sherman when Napoleon Daniels took the mound for the Twins; but his operation was independent. It was the Browns' practice to send those players out in pairs "because they can be together, live together and in general be happier with an organization." O'dell Hightower would have the distinction of being the only black Hereford. Like the 1953 team, the 1954 edition was all-white. Regarding pro-moting the team, management took a page from the 1952 K-O-M League team in Independence, Kansas. A one-day sale of ten admissions for $4.95 would be the solution. On March 3, the Ada Base-ball Association set up a booth at Main and Broad-way and began selling cards that, like a meal ticket, could be punched for each admission. An individ-ual could attend ten separate games or a group of ten could go in on one card. Some eight-hundred cards were sold.

Following spring training at the Browns' mi-nor league camp at Thomasville, Georgia, Brower brought his team to Ada. The 1953 edition had five returnees from 1952: right fielder James Cumbie, outfielder Larry Burford, catcher Mike Goffredo, relief catcher Doc McCarn, pitcher Neil Thode, and shortstop Ron Slawski. Outfielder Tony Costa and first baseman Bob Norden as veterans had "national service" status and did not count against

1953 Ada Herefords. L-R: Top row: Manager Lou Brower*, George Werrmann*, Ron Slawski*, Toni Costa*, Bob Norden*, Lloyd Bohn, Neil Thode*, J.L. Rhodes*, Chico Gonzales*, Jim Miller. Front row: Pablo Labrador, Doc McCarn*, Ron Coburn, Don McGregor*, Bob Bonebrake, George Blash*, Buddy Yount, Ross Sergo. Batboys: Bill Thrash and Bob Cornell. Not pictured: Ron Pitre. (* Played at Ada in 1952 or were on opening day roster.) Burford and Higgins were reassigned. Goffredo and Williams earned promotions during the season. Cumbie and Albert were released. Bohn, Bonebrake, Miller, and Coburn were signed as rookies. Sergo was sent down from Pine Bluff. Labrador and Yount were veterans picked up to bolster the pitching staff for the playoffs.

Elwanda Morgan, left, and Ann Noe were among the fans taking advantage of the one-day pre-season sale.

the fifteen player limit. Infielder Chico Gonzalez was the other limited service player. The rest were rookies: catcher-outfielder George Blash, shortstop Canadian Don McGregor, and hurlers J. L. Rhodes, Earl Higgins, Bill Williams, Bob Albert, George Werrmann, and Reg Pitre. Cline Fowler was hired as business manager.

The Herefords dropped the April 21, 1953 season opener at McAlester four to three with Ada taking the second before returning to Hereford Park. The scheduled April 23 opener was rained out. The following day's twin bill before 1,500 saw Ron Slawski's grand slam propel the Herefords to an eight to four win for Ron Pitre's first victory. Rocket pitcher Ron Saatzer won the nightcap for himself with the second grand slam of the day. After dropping a pair to the Twins and Shawnee at home, Ada vanquished the Dodgers' farmhands

Manager Lou Brower, center, hugs his game-winners Tony Costa (left) and Chico Gonzalez.

Ad for twin bill with Cincinnati's rookies at Lawton.

Ada's moundsmen for the 1953 playoffs. L-R: J. L. "Dusty" Rhodes, Pablo Labrador, Ron Coburn, Lloyd Bohn, George Werrmann, Neil Thode, Ross Sergo, and Buddy Yount.

from Shawnee sixteen to seven behind Norden and Slawski's roundtrippers in a game that saw twenty-eight hits and nine errors. Rookie J. L. Rhodes had five hitless innings before a four-run sixth to drop the following night's decision. The wins continued.

Catcher Mike Goffredo preserved J.L. Rhodes' two-hit shutout on May 14 against Lawton by tagging Lawton catcher Harold Ridley after his teammates carried him off the field to the dugout in celebration of the Reds' first homer of the season; their enthusiasm prevented him from touching home plate. Ridley was credited with a triple. The Herefords took the second game on James Cumbie's RBI to give Werrmann another win. When Sherman-Denison came to play the next evening, a television was set up in Hereford Park so that the fans would not miss the heavyweight fight between Rocky Marciano and Jersey Joe Walcott. When McAlester

returned to town, Tony Costa's grand slam and Chico Gonzalez's walk off double moved the Herefords into first place with a thirteen to twelve victory.

On June 18 the Adans were in first place, two games ahead of Ardmore and still in front a month later. A slump over the next fortnight found the Herefords in fourth but only one and one-half game out of second. With eighteen days remaining in the season, third place looked like a lock with Ada leading McAlester by four games. On August 8, they had blasted Sherman-Denison twenty to five also with seven home runs including three in the first inning by Don McGregor, Ron Slawski, and George Blash.

Unofficial final tallies showed Ada in a second-place tie with Shawnee; post-season adjustments would drop the Herefords to third, one and one-half games behind the Hawks.

Ada eliminated Shawnee in four games and then fell to nemesis McAlester four games to one in Ada's only appearance in the playoff finals. At .270, the 1953 Herefords led the League in team batting, and were tops with 1,997 total bases, and 147 home runs. Ada pitchers posted the League's best with 996 strike outs. Fielding was weak once more but pitching improved markedly. It all added up to a third place finish and Ada's last trip to the playoffs. Bob Norden and Ron Slawski tied for the League lead in home runs with thirty-one apiece. Rhodes led all Sooner State League pitchers with twenty-one wins. The staff posted a group ERA of 4.18 with Reggie Pitre leading the team at 2.63 in 106 innings. The highest ERA on the staff was only 4.46 by Lloyd Bohn.

1954

The Browns became the Baltimore Orioles soon after the end of the 1953 season. The relocation was a surprise to no one. Seller Bill Veeck had

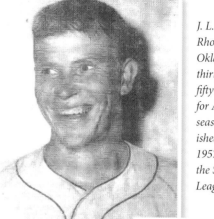

J. L. "Dusty" Rhodes of Pierce, Oklahoma won thirty-nine of fifty-eight decisions for Ada in two seasons. He finished his career in 1957 with Paris in the Sooner State League.

Charles "Buddy" Yount won seventeen games for McAlester in 1948 before service in Korea and a sore arm. He appeared for Ada at the end of 1953 and returned for 1954 after Paris released him. His pitching was never the same after his combat tour in Korea with the Oklahoma National Guard.

been trying to move the St. Louis American League franchise since the day he bought the team. The move did not change the relationship with Ada. The working agreement was to remain in force for the 1954 season. Poor advance sales of advertising and season tickets were a harbinger of problems to come in 1954. Sanford tried with little success to obtain $3,000 in limited liability notes, essentially partial guaranties, from investors and civic leaders to finance the season.

With sophomore staff ace J.L. Rhodes and .364 hitting veteran Doc McCarn returning for his third season at Ada, manager Brower hoped to match the performance of his 1953 Herefords with the rookies and limited service players sent from the Orioles' minor league camp. With the exception of Rhodes and Russell Gramlow, released after his only decision, all the pitchers were rookies: James Wolcott, Jan Christensen, Roman Schultheis, and Rich Tait; Russ McDonald and Rueben Saager had seen limited action in under forty-five innings in 1953 to maintain rookie status. First sacker Ron Barbian, who had been in the A's organization in 1953, and Harold Norton, released after eight games, were the only limited service players. Catchers Ed Brundick and Ralph Vulpitta, infielders Jack Whereatte, Ken Hinton, and John Densmore and outfielders Bruce Lane and Rich Lubinski were rookies. None of the 1954 Herefords were veterans.

Left hander Rhodes got Lou Brower's second season at the helm off to a good start with an eight nil, six-hit shutout over McAlester. Nearly ten percent of the season's attendance, 2,674, showed up in the season-opening win. After that, average game attendance was only 300-350. Play was sporadic, though, due to weather. Ada had six rainouts in the first month of the season. Ada exploited

doormat Pauls Valley. In one contest Rich Lubinski's three-run homer provided the difference in the Herefords' fourteen to eleven win. In another, Russ McDonald sent thirteen Raiders to the dugout with bats in hand.

The Herefords nearly pulled off a win against Shawnee on May 6, despite George Green holding them to one hit, when they scored five runs on seven walks and five errors; Shawnee held on to win six to five. On May 22, the Herefords extracted some revenge by tattooing Hawk hurler Walt Callahan for eleven hits and taking thirteen walks in route to a fifteen to one blow out. Two days later, on May 24, John DeSousa gave up a League record-tying five triples to Shawnee dropping a twelve to seven decision. At that point, the Adans were tied with Lawton for sixth place having won fourteen of thirty-one starts, just one game out of fifth. A month later they were playing .500 ball and clinging to

Rich Lubinski (1935-) was back in the Sooner State League with Paris in 1956.

Catcher Ed Brudnick (left) and first sacker Ron Barbian (right) contributed home runs to Dusty Rhodes' season-opening win.

BELOW: "Hot" Rod Kanehl (1934-2004) was an original member of the New York Mets in 1962 where he played every position but pitcher and catcher. He played two more seasons before retiring. He was the only Met to attend Casey Stengal's funeral in 1975. He owned a restaurant in Palm Springs where he died at age seventy.

ABOVE: Russ McDonald (1935-) had a record of twenty-two wins against thirty-two losses in the Orioles' organization. He finished with Stockton in the Class C California League.

Slugger Walt Massefski (1935-) played his entire career in the Browns/Orioles organization. He was the only 1954 Cementer to appear the next season with Paris.

fourth place with McAlester one-half game behind. Ada had the distinction of allowing McAlester's Rod Kanehl five hits in five trips on July 4, for his thirty-second consecutive game with a hit to set the Sooner State League record.

The Herefords' team batting average of .285 was topped only by the .300 of the 1950 champions. The 1954 edition was the most iron-gloved of a franchise with a history of poor fielding. With thirty-nine passed balls and 432 errors, the Adans fielded .922. The pitchers were seventh in the League with a collective ERA of 5.53 and leader in gopher balls with 176. Rhodes again was the ace at 3.82 ERA supporting a winning eighteen versus thirteen record. The sole All-Star who wore a Hereford uniform, Walt Massefski, picked up after

Cementers Romp Past Braves, Seminole Oilers Here Tonight

The city of Ada quickly adopted its new ball club.

being cut from Gainesville in May, was the leading hitter at .363 with seventeen home runs. Rich Lubinski had the most home runs with twenty-eight. Rhodes, who had thirty-nine wins against nineteen losses after his second season, again was the ace of the staff even though serving up thirty-two homers.

Before July 31, Sanford had made the three prior $1,750 semi-monthly payrolls out of his own pocket. He was unwilling to do so a fourth time. The players went unpaid. Baltimore terminated its working agreement with Ada and released most of its players under contract. Unable to get anyone to pay the $10,000 asking price for the Herefords, on that same day, Ada Baseball Association, Inc. surrendered its franchise to the Sooner State League and the remaining players became League property.

From the opening day roster, outfielders Lubinski, Vulpitta and Hinton, first baseman Barbian, Adan Doc McCarn, and Rhodes remained. Other Cementers included utility man Massefski, rookie second baseman James Samford, infielder Allan Bailey acquired from Seminole, third sacker Harlie Page sent down from York of the Piedmont League, pitchers John DeSousa and Don Cartwright on loan from the Orioles' Americus, Georgia farm club, and hurler Dale Kingma returned from Aberdeen of the Northern League. Fern Smathers, fresh from class at Southeastern Oklahoma State College, secured the first string catcher's position at mid-season hitting at a torrid .429 pace before dropping to .323 at season end. Another late signee, Darrell Newhouse, joined the pitchers for sixteen games.

For two days, the League itself operated the

team as the Ada "Sooner States." Meanwhile, with a $1,750 subsidy from the League's treasury to cover the missed payroll, Charles Mayfield, owner of an Ada oilfield cementing firm, took over the franchise operations as Ada Athletic Association, Inc., and changed the team's name to "Cementers." He kept Cline Fowler in the front office. He fired Lou Brower and hired Ada service station operator Jerry Densmore, not to be confused with rookie third baseman John Densmore, to assume field command. In his only prior foray into professional baseball, manager Densmore had hit .197 in seventeen games for the 1950 Herefords. He was not able to lift the new Cementers to the first division, nor did attendance pick up.

The pickup Cementers won eighteen of forty-four under new management. Ada went out of Organized Baseball with a whimper, losing its last game to McAlester eight to four to finish twenty-eight games off the pace. The sixth-place team drew 28,482 for the season.

Mayfield claimed that the problem with the Ada team all along had been the hook up with the Browns/Orioles. He had created bad blood and it was a certainty Ada would not be in the Orioles'1955 farm system. Despite his best efforts following the season, Mayfield was unable to obtain a working agreement with any other team at the Major League Winter Meeting. The Orioles, and with them the Major Leagues, had blacklisted Ada in general and Charles Mayfield in particular. The franchise was turned back on December 26, 1954. The only baseball played in 1955 was sandlot.

CLASS D

OFFICIAL NOTICE OF DISPOSITION OF PLAYER'S CONTRACT AND SERVICES

National Association of Professional Baseball Leagues

MAIL ONE NOTICE AT ONCE TO: (1) President National Association.
(2) President of your League.
(3) Hand one to player. (If not possible, mail copy to player by registered mail.)
(4) Retain one copy for your files.

October 1, 1954

(Date)

TO PLAYER Fern D. Smathers _____. You are hereby officially notified of the following disposition of your contract:

Your contract has this date been assigned outright to the Cordele Club of the Georgia-Florida League.

Ada _____ Club _____ Sooner State _____ League

By _____ Bus Mgr. _____ (Title)

(CLUB WILL SELECT APPROPRIATE STATEMENT FROM LIST BELOW AND TYPE OR PRINT ENTIRE STATEMENT ABOVE)

(a) You are released outright and unconditionally.
(b) Your contract has this date been assigned outright to the _____ (Club Name) Club of the _____ (League Name) League.
(c) Your contract has this date been conditionally assigned to the _____ (Club Name) Club of the _____ (League Name) League.
(d) Your contract has this date been optionally assigned to the _____ (Club Name) Club of the _____ (League Name) League.
(e) Your contract has this date been returned to the _____ (Club Name) Club of the _____ (League Name) League.
(f) Your contract has this date been assigned to the _____ (Club Name) Club of the _____ (League Name) League, subject to the option of _____ (Club Name) Club of the _____ (League Name) League.
(g) The right to recall your contract has this date been cancelled by the _____ (Club Name) Club of the _____ (League Name) League.
(h) Your contract has this date been recalled by the _____ (Club Name) Club of the _____ (League Name) League.

DO NOT WRITE IN BOX

DO NOT WRITE IN BOX

RECEIPT

_____ (Date)

RECEIPT OF COPY OF THIS OFFICIAL NOTICE IS ACKNOWLEDGED

_____ (Player)

Place X in box if player is sent copy by REGISTERED mail.

☒ PLAYER SENT COPY OF THIS OFFICIAL NOTICE BY REGISTERED MAIL.

Baseball players were essentially chattels. They could accept the sale of their contracts and move to a new team or quit the game. Cline Fowler signed the Notice to Fern Smathers that he had been assigned outright to Cordele, Georgia, of the Georgia-Florida League.

CHAPTER TWO

HEREFORD PARK

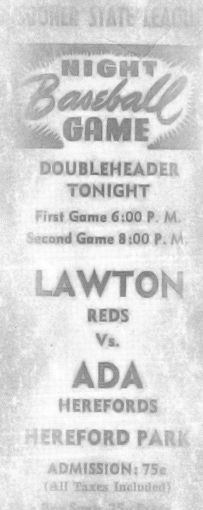

"A rabbit would have to pack a lunch to walk across the field."

—CHARLIE HOPKINS, Catcher 1948

The Ada firefighters put on a rodeo in the middle of the Great Depression as a fundraiser. Held at the old Ada ball park on West Main, it was more successful than they could have imagined. A 150-foot long concrete and steel grandstand for a rodeo area was built in 1938 by the Works Progress Administration near the northeast corner of 18th and Broadway across from the Armory, also a WPA project. Ada's semi-pro team, the Independents, made a contribution in the form of lighting from the old park. In 1940, a roof was placed over the stands. An additional 125 feet of grandstand was added in 1942 to increase capacity to 2,500. By the end of World War II, the Ada Rodeo was second in size only to Cheyenne, Wyoming's Frontier Days among outdoor rodeos. Ada was the capital of Hereford Heaven and to show that a large statue of a Hereford was placed at the Pontotoc County Fairgrounds near the rodeo arena. Bleachers were added every year to bring total capacity to 12,000. After a season of Sooner State League play, the *Ada Evening News* opined on May 27, 1948 "you can't mix rodeo performance and baseball games on the same field."

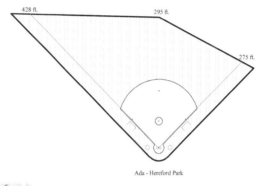

Ada - Hereford Park

The original 1938 grandstand. An additional 125 feet and a roof were added during World War II to increase the capacity to 2,500.

The configuration was among the strangest in Organized Baseball. It was ideal for left-handed batters who could pull the ball. The Herefords led the Sooner State League in home run production in 1947, 1948, 1950, 1952, and 1953.

A view of the grandstand than ran parallel to the first base line.

The Hopkins family by the south club-house side of Hereford Park.

That, however, is exactly where the Ada Herefords played home games during their eight seasons. The rodeo grounds forced an awkward configuration. The field was completely bare dirt. From home plate to the left field fence was 428 feet. The right field fence at the end of the grandstand was a short 275 feet away while center field was a mere twenty feet further than the right field line. The grandstand ran parallel to the first base line with home plate at the northeast end. There were bull chutes in center field. Bleachers stood beyond the right field fence and along the left field line. The fence from center field to the left field foul pole ran parallel to 18th Street. The lighting was notoriously poor. The sports editor of the *Seminole Producer* commented "why elderly men and long term married couples pay admission price to go out [to Hereford Park] and sit in the dark is beyond me."

Hereford Park was to be a bane as long as the team played there. For ten days in early August, the Herefords had to become a road team as the annual Ada Rodeo was going on. Baseball home games were then played in nearby Sulphur. After the Herefords moved to Paris, American Legion and sandlot teams occupied Hereford Park. The Agri-Plex, a modern indoor arena, stands where Hereford Park was located.

Mack Hyde stands by the west end of the "dugout."

The bleachers along the third base side are visible behind Bobby King in this 1948 photo.

The Herefords' "dugout" was on the third base side. As there was no plumbing, the players shared a water bucket.

CHAPTER THREE

ADA OWNERS, MANAGERS, AND PLAYERS

Dr. A. R. Sugg
• Co-Owner 1947-1948

With Edwin Free, later to be an organizer and first business manager of the Chickasha club, Dr. Albert Roscoe Sugg, Sr. (1895-1961) and Ucal Clanton formed Ada Baseball Club, Inc. with a $10,000 capitalization. Dr. Sugg was the leading physician in Ada, and had chaired the Chamber of Commerce in 1940. Sugg was president of the local semi-pro team, the Ada Independents, before World War II. That team moved to the new Fairgrounds grandstand in 1938 when the old ball park on West Main was torn down. Ada was the first franchise to obtain a Major League working agreement. The relationship with the St. Louis Browns and later the Baltimore Orioles was to last until the last month of the franchise's existence in Ada.

With Sugg providing money and boosting the team locally and Ucal Clanton leading the team on the field, the Herefords showed a profit in 1947 boasting attendance of 41,872 and a third-place finish in a six-team league. In 1948, however, they saw the previous

The Sugg Clinic is one of the most outstanding models of Streamline Moderne architecture. A medical clinic from 1947 to 1980, it is presently an office building.

Before the 1953 season, meeting with the new manager. L-R: Manager Lou Brower, Directors Luther Edge, Guy Thrash, Lawrence Sanford,and Promotions Manager Monte Bell.

year's operating profit evaporate as a fifth-place team finished 63-76 before 27,050. In October, 1948, Sugg and Clanton sold their stock to Ada Ford dealer, Robert W. Cason, Jr.

Dr. Sugg built one of the most architecturally forward-looking clinics in Oklahoma. He served as president of the Oklahoma Medical Association in 1952. He died in Ada on December 17, 1961.

Robert W. Cason, Jr.
- **Owner 1949-1951**

World War II fighter pilot and Ford dealer Bob Cason (1918-1992) was a hands-on owner, attending spring training at the Browns' Minor League facility in Pine Bluff, Arkansas and was involved with selection of the manager of the St. Louis farm-hands. A weak team in 1949 made his first season as owner a financial disappointment. Despite a regular season pennant in 1950, attendance failed to pick up much over 1949, just 4,931 to 31,981, when the Herefords finished fourth in the League. Bleeding cash in 1951 when only 12,779 saw Stan Galle's fifth-place Herefords, Cason cut bait. He handed over the team to another local group.

Lawrence Sanford, Jr.
- **Owner 1952 - July 31, 1954**

Oilman Lawrence Sanford, Jr. (1927-2004) and Kaiser-Frazer automobile dealer Guy Thrash, whose son Bill served as batboy in 1952 and 1953, assembled a group that capitalized Ada Baseball Association, Inc. with $25,000 in March, 1952, to purchase the assets of Ada Baseball Club, Inc. which had held the franchise since 1947. While successful at raising attendance in 1952 and 1953, they were unable to stanch the outflow of cash. Operating losses in those years impaired capital. Pre-season ticket and advertising sales for 1954 lagged. Pledges of limited financial guaranties for 1954 were not honored.

Sanford dug deep into his own pocket to make three payrolls. By the end of July, with attendance averaging around 325 and unable to find the $3,500 needed to complete the season, the Sanford group could no longer sustain the losses. When the parent Orioles terminated the working agreement, Ada Baseball Association, Inc. turned the franchise back to the League on August 1. The dean of Sooner State League managers, Lou Brower, was released, and the contracts of players who had not been Baltimore property belonged to the League.

Charles Mayfield
• **Owner July 31- December 9, 1954**

Oil well servicer Charles Mayfield (1918-2011) was waiting in the wings as the Ada ball club was sinking. When the franchise was turned back to the League, he offered to take over the operation. He incorporated Ada Athletic Association, Inc. with $10,000 capital, on August 3, and along with a $1,750 subsidy from the League to cover the most recently missed payroll, christened his team the Ada Cementers. They would hold the field for the remainder of the season. At season's end, he told the players to keep the Herefords uniforms. The team would have new ones for 1955.

Mayfield worked diligently to secure a Major League working agreement but had made an enemy of the Orioles' minor league development office. The day of independent minor league teams was drawing to a close and Major League clubs were consolidating their minor league systems. After three days at the December, 1954, Major League Owners' Meeting, he could not garner any interest from any team. Mayfield notified the League that he could not operate in 1955. The Cementers became a sandlot team. Not without some controversy, the Sooner State League moved the Ada franchise to Paris, Texas.

Ucal "Uke" Clanton
• **Co-Owner and Manager 1947 and 1948**

Nicknamed "the Cat," he had a great glove but lacked the eye to hit Big League pitching. His highest classification was in the AA Southern Association with the New Orleans Pelicans and Little Rock Travelers in 1923. He finished his professional playing days with the Shawnee Robins of the Western Association in 1930 hitting .299.

Clanton played sandlot ball in the Shawnee area for the Yoder Merchants and Blackwell Oilers as well as for the Antlers Mountaineers, appearing at first base in the state tourney in 1930. He managed and played first base for the Shawnee Oilers tourney teams in 1933 and 1936, taking the latter to the state championship. He managed and played for Ada's semi-pro Independents after 1936.

Clanton lettered in baseball at the University of Oklahoma in 1916. After two seasons with Muskogee, he was called up for a one -game appearance with Cleveland in September, 1922. Ucal "Uke" Clanton (1898-1960) played the next eight seasons as a minor league first baseman and later led the Ada Independents semi-pro club.

Clanton helped organize the Sooner State League in 1946 and was part owner and manager of the Ada Herefords in 1947 and 1948. He lived in Ada and owned and operated an insurance agency while scouting for the White Sox, Browns, and Braves after 1948. Clanton was elected Sooner State League president at the fall 1951 annual meeting, ousting Jack Mealey. He umpired during the 1940s and 1950s and established an umpiring school with Dutch Prather in 1955. Commander of the local American Legion Post and president of the Ada Elks Club, he was active in Ada's youth baseball programs. Clanton was killed in a one-car accident six miles west of Antlers, Oklahoma, at age fifty-seven on February 20, 1960.

Bill Krueger

- **Manager 1949 and 1950.**

The North Carolina native began his professional career with Fond du Lac, Wisconsin, in 1941. He missed 1942 and 1945, but managed to spend 1943 and 1944 with Portland, Seattle, and Sacramento of the Pacific Coast League. His hitting was not enough to keep him at the AAA level when the World War II veterans returned in 1946. Signed to a St. Louis Browns contract, he played at Idaho Falls, Modesto and Willows, California, before being appointed player-manager for the Herefords in 1949. He took his 1949 team to a sixty-nine win fourth-place finish then won the 1950 regular season race. He had his best playing years at Ada hitting .349 with twenty-one home runs and ninety-eight RBIs in 1950. He holds the all-time Sooner State League record for most grand slams—four in a season. Called up for the Korean Conflict, he missed 1951 and 1952. Krueger finished his career in the Browns/Orioles organization managing Thedford Mines, Quebec, in the Provincial League, Aberdeen S.D. of the Northern League, and Texas City in the 1956 Big State League race.

Stan Galle (1919-2006) coached the baseball team of Spring Hill College in Mobile, Alabama, for twenty-four years (1958-1982). The baseball field there is the oldest in the United States —in use since 1888. It was named for Galle following his retirement.

Stan Galle

- **Manager 1951.**

Born Stanley Galaczewski in Milwaukee, he began his professional career directly out of high school. He played for his hometown Brewers in the American Association in 1939, 1940, and 1941. Following his Major League career of only sixteen games in early 1942 with the Washington Senators, he returned to the Association with the Toledo Mudhens. After the War, he rejoined the Mudhens before finishing 1946 with the Browns' San Antonio Missions of the Texas League. He did not play from 1947 to 1950. He tried his hand at managing the Herefords in 1951 where he hit .317. His team did not do as well, finishing fifth before 12, 700 fans, the lowest in Ada history.

1952'S THREE MANAGERS

Bill Enos • (Spring Training-August 5)

Enos (1920-) had an undistinguished playing career principally in the St. Louis Browns' organization rising to Class B with the Miami Sun Sox and West Palm Beach Indians of the Florida Interna-

Bill Krueger (1922-)

Enos handing out meal money.

Enos later was inducted into the Cape Cod League Hall of Fame as a scout. The cigar is his trademark.

tional League. He began managing in 1949 with Mayfield, Kentucky, of the Class D Kitty League and continued to work with Browns' prospects at places such as Pittsburg, Kansas, of the K-O-M League and Pine Bluff, Arkansas, home of the Browns' minor league training center, in the Cotton States League. 1954 was his last year in uniform.

In 1955 he became, at age thirty-two, the youngest scout in Organized Baseball, first with the Kansas City A's, and later with the Brewers and Red Sox scouring New England for new talent. He was inducted into the Cape Cod Baseball League Hall of Fame in 2001. At Ada, his Browns farmhands began the season in the first division but by August 5, the day he was released by the Ada ownership, the Herefords had sunk to seventh place. A team 6.00 ERA and .938 fielding average are indicative of the talent on hand.   Enos soon joined the front office in St. Louis.

Virl Loman • (August 4-15)
He managed the Herefords for two weeks following Enos. He completed his playing career with the Seminole Oilers in 1950 where he won ten of twenty-six decisions. He ran a Texaco station at the corner of Main and Mississippi in Ada during and after his playing days. He appeared in ten games for the 1952 Herefords during his eleven-game tenure losing two decisions. Unable to manage as a volunteer and keep his business going, he stepped down. Without a manager for a second time, the Ada front office turned to someone that already was under contract to finish the season, its nineteen-year-old second baseman.

Jim England • (August 16-Season End)
With Bill Enos standing as his best man, he and bride Joan had been married in Ada at the beginning of the season. 1952 was England's best year in baseball hitting .324 with 198 hits in 612 at bats. He holds the all time Sooner State League record for the most at bats. He played two more years then

Virl Loman (1910-1993) was a local from Union Valley, Oklahoma, who in two full seasons (1948-1949), five games in 1950, and ten in 1952 compiled a record of twenty-one wins against seventeen losses for Ada.

James R. England (1932-), in only his second year of professional baseball, took over the team for the last ten days of the season; in seventh place they had no hope of post-season play.

was released after a .180 season at Class B Keokuk, Iowa, of the Three-I League.

Lou Brower
• **Manager 1953-August 1, 1954.**

Brower led Lawton for its first four years, 1947-1950, finishing first, second, second, and eighth respectively. The 1949 team won the Shaughnessy playoff.   He was at the helm of Pauls Valley in 1951, its last year as an independent, and 1952, the first season as a farm club, and managed the Browns-Orioles farm team at Ada in 1953 and in 1954 until the working agreement was cancelled and the team sold. He took the 1953 Herefords to the playoff finals losing to Shawnee in five games. As he departed in 1954, he observed that the officiating in the Sooner State League was the worst he had seen in his baseball career.

Born Isadore Harold Brower, Lou "Old Folks" Brower (1900-1994) came out of retirement to manage three Sooner State League teams between 1947 and 1954.

Of fourteen seasons as an active player, Brower spent nine with the Oklahoma City Indians both in the Western League and Texas League. As a shortstop, he was named to the 1927 Western League All-Star team as well as the 1935 Texas League stars. Along with fellow Sooner State League manager Ed Marleau, he was a member of the 1935 Dixie Series champions who defeated Atlanta of the Southern Association four games to two. He also played at Tulsa of the Texas League, Little Rock of the Southern Association, and began his managerial career with Waterloo, Iowa, of the Three-I League in 1941. A weak-hitting (.161) Major League shortstop, he played in twenty-one games with Detroit during the 1931 season before being sent to Toronto. He has an entry in the *Big Book of Jewish Baseball*. He died on March 4, 1994, at Tyler, Texas, and is buried in Memorial Park Cemetery in Oklahoma City.

Jerry Densmore
- **Manager Ada Cementers August 3-Season End, 1954.**

Densmore was the last professional baseball manager in the history of the Ada franchise. When Baltimore pulled its working agreement because it appeared that the franchise would fold, manager Lou Brower was fired. New owner Charles Mayfield appointed local third baseman Jerry Densmore. Like Kelly Wingo, who had played and managed in the Sooner State League between 1949 and 1951, he had been a star athlete at Shawnee High School. He had spent his only season in Organized Baseball as a light-hitting infielder (.197) in seventeen games for the 1950 Ada Herefords.

Joe Wood , Jr.
- **Pitcher 1947.**

Son of Hall of Fame pitcher "Smokey Joe" Wood, at age twenty-eight during the first two weeks of May, 1944, he played in three games for the Boston Red Sox posting a record of no wins and one loss with a 6.52 ERA. He had played at Yale under his father who was the varsity coach. He began throwing professionally in 1941 and spent the time before appearing at Fenway Park at the Boston farm clubs at Scranton and Louisville. Following being released, Wood signed with San Diego of the Pacific Coast League for the remainder of 1944. He had losing records for Sacramento in 1945 and 1946 before being sent down to Class C Fresno at the end of July, 1946. Released again, he signed with Ada and then was sold to Seminole.

Forest "Woody" Smith
- **Pitcher 1947.**

Smith had yet to acquire the nickname "Woody" while he was in the Sooner State League. He was in his second year in professional baseball when he was selected to be an All-Star for leading

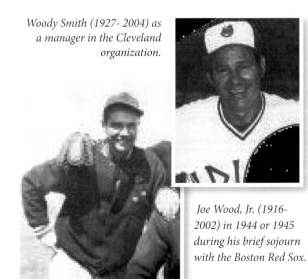

Woody Smith (1927- 2004) as a manager in the Cleveland organization.

Joe Wood, Jr. (1916-2002) in 1944 or 1945 during his brief sojourn with the Boston Red Sox.

the second-place Herefords and the League with twenty-three wins, a winning percentage at .690 and an ERA of 2.00. He pitched his best, and as it turned out his last, game on August 29, against Seminole facing only thirty-one batters while giving up four hits and striking out nine; he faced no more than four Oilers in any inning. The eight nil shutout was his twenty-third victory. He also hit the ball averaging .286 in 140 at bats pinch hitting and playing left field.

After sitting out 1948 with a sore arm, the Browns assigned him to their Class C Gloversville-Johnstown club in the Canadian-American League where he learned the third base position and hit .324 and .288 in his two seasons there. He was drafted by the Yankees and played three seasons at Beaumont and AAA Kansas City before being traded in 1954 to the Phillies' top club at Syracuse of the International League in 1954. After a 1955 detour in the American Association with the hapless independent Charleston Senators, he was to call the International League home for the rest of his playing career. After 103 games with Havana—where he became acquainted with Fidel Castro—he spent the remainder of 1956 with the Miami Marlins whose pitching staff included Satchel Paige. He was an All-Star at third base for the Marlins between 1957 and 1960 and the Miami MVP for three consecutive seasons.

He earned a Silver Glove as the best fielding third sacker in Minor League baseball and along the way the moniker "Mr. Reliable." When the Marlins moved to San Juan in 1961, Smith joined Syracuse, then a Minnesota farm club, for the second time. He finished in the same organization with which he began, playing in ten games with the Orioles' Rochester club. He managed Miami's entry in the Florida State League between 1969 and 1972 winning the pennant each year. When the Orioles let him go in 1973, he joined the Cleveland organization manag-

ing their teams at San Antonio in 1974 and 1975, Waterloo, Iowa for 1977 and 1978, and Chattanooga between 1979 and 1981. He later scouted. He died in February, 2004.

Bill Donaghey
• **Pitcher 1947, 1950.**

Blind in his right eye, Donaghey (1922-1998), a half Choctaw Indian from Sasakwa, Oklahoma, teamed with Forest Smith to lead the inaugural edition of the Herefords, contributing twenty-two wins against seven losses. After spending 1948 and 1949 with the Browns' Class C clubs at Globe-Miami, El Paso, and Muskogee, he was back in Ada in 1950 for his last professional season going out on top with a record of twenty-six wins in thirty-one decisions. He led the League in strike outs with 244 in 1947 and in 1950 led in wins and winning percentage as well as being named to the All-Star team. At Globe-Miami of the Arizona-Texas League he won fourteen and lost eight in 1948 and pitched .500 ball in 1949 with thirteen apiece. He settled in Artesia, N.M. He died there on August 12, 1998.

Steve Molinari
• **Outfielder 1949-1950.**

Appearing in thirteen games for the 1949 Herefords, in 1950 he did a complete turnaround from his .125 and one home run performance. In addi-

Originally assigned to Seminole by the White Sox, after only nine games Molinari (1931-) was sold to the Browns along with Bill Milligan and sent down the road to their Ada farm club.

tion to setting the Sooner State League record with thirty-nine home runs, he hit .360 with 162 RBIs, best in the league. That earned him a promotion to Class C Pine Bluff of the Cotton States League for 1951 where he led that league with 106 RBIs and twenty-four home runs. He jumped to Class A Scranton of the Eastern League for 1952 with .257, nineteen home runs, and seventy-six RBIs.

His career was detoured for two seasons in the service where he played for the Army at Ft. Dix in New Jersey. Returning in 1954, the Orioles sent him to Class A Wichita of the Western League where he was hitting .289 with only one home run when sent down to Class C Aberdeen S.D. of the Northern League, closer to his home in Williston, N.D. He began 1956 with the Orioles' Class B team at Lubbock. Released outright in June, he signed with the independent Victoria Eagles in the Big State League and then moved south of the border for the remainder of the season with Monterrey and Nuevo Laredo of the Mexican League.

Molinari retired from Organized Baseball but became a member of the semi-pro Williston Oilers of the ManDak League in 1957. An automobile accident ended his playing days. He worked in the meat packing business in Williston.

Fern Smathers
• Catcher 1954.

Denison, Texas native Fern Smathers signed with the Browns late in the 1953 season and played twenty-eight games for Valdosta in the Georgia-Florida League. Classified as a rookie at Ada in 1954, the young catcher saw little action until starting catcher Ed Brundick, hitting an anemic .205, was released on July 15. Smathers took off like a roman candle hitting a torrid .452 in his first thirty-one at bats. He came down to earth by the end of the season but managed a .323 average with

Fern Smathers (1934-) models his 1947-1948 vintage Herefords uniform. When Ada became the Cementers on August 2, the new owner decided to defer purchase of flannels with the new name. After the season, Cementers owner Charles Mayfield told the players that they could keep their uniforms.

a .460 slugging percentage. His fielding was near the top of the League at .977 but did not reflect thirteen passed balls. The Orioles assigned him to their Class D Cordele, Georgia team.

His performance in 1955 spring drills, though, earned him a promotion to Aberdeen of the Class C Northern League. A .310 average early in the season saw him sent up to York of the Class B Piedmont League. In twenty-seven games there, he hit .244 and was dealt to Thedford Mines in the Class C Provincial League. While a good glove man, his hitting declined in 1956 with Columbus of the Sally League. He deviated from the usual pattern for players detoured by a couple of years in the military. Missing the 1957 and 1958 seasons, the Orioles tested his potential with Amarillo of the Class AA Texas League for 1959 and he responded with a .304 performance, even after laying out a month with an injury.

For 1960, the O's placed him on the roster of their top farm club in Vancouver, B.C. of the Pacific Coast League. With American League All-Star Gus Triandos ensconced in Baltimore, a surplus of catchers such as bonus baby Frank Zupo in the farm system, and only one AAA team, Baltimore loaned Smathers to the Victoria Rosebuds for the 1960 campaign where he was manager Johnny Pesky's regular catcher. Off-season he pursued his education, earning a B.S. degree from Southeastern State College in Durant. Sheepskin in hand, he traded himself from the Orioles to Dupont Co. Today he lives in Baton Rouge with his wife Joanna, a native of Ardmore, where they are active in the ministry of the Believers' Club.

KIDS

The players were close to the fans, especially the children.

Young Bobby King drew a young admirer in 1948.

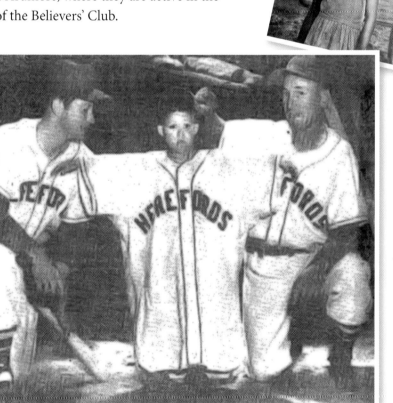

Before the 1953 season, James Cumbie (left) and manager Lou Brower (right) help four-year-old Gregg Taylor into a Hereford's jersey.

CHAPTER FOUR

HEREFORDS' BESTS

EIGHT SEASON RECORD:
573 wins • 536 losses • 6 ties • .517 winning percentage

SOONER STATE LEAGUE RECORDS

Games in One Season: 143 in 1949 (tie with McAlester)

Most Runs in One Inning: 17 versus Lawton; 1949

Most Home Runs/Game: 7 on August 16, 1952

Most Grand Slams/Season: 10 in 1954

Most Grand Slams/Game: 2 in 1950 (tied with two others)

Highest Slugging Percentage: .487 in 1950

Most Complete Games by Pitchers: 95 in 1950

Most Hits Allowed: 1,483 in 1954

Most Home Runs Allowed: 176 in 1954

Most Balks in One Season: 28 in 1952

Most Bases on Balls in One Season: 1,068 in 1952

Most Pitchers in a Single Game: 7 on July 13, 1952

Most Put Outs in One Season: 3,802 in 1948

Most Triple Plays: 2 in 1948 (tied with two others)

Most Errors/Game: 9 on August 25, 1947 and July 9, 1951

SOONER STATE LEAGUE INDIVIDUAL RECORDS

At Bats: 612 • **James England**; 1952

Home Runs: 39 • **Steve Molinari**; 1950 (tied with one other)

Runs Batted In: 162 • **Steve Molinari**; 1950

Runs in One Game: 6 • **Dennis Rackley**; 1948 (tied with three others)

Hits in One Inning: 3 • **Fred Boiko**; 1949 (2 singles, 1 home run)

Grand Slams in One Season: 4 • **Bill Krueger**; 1950

Fewest Strike Outs in One Season: 7 • **Bill Enos**; 1952

Most Errors in One Game: 6 • **Stuart Chestnut**; 1949

Most 20-game seasons: 2 • **Bill Donaghey** (1947 and 1950)

Most Runs Allowed in One Season: 226 • **James Harper**; 1951

Most Earned Runs Allowed in One Season: 172 • **James Harper**; 1951

Most Bases on Balls in One Game: 21 • **James Harper**; 1951

ALL-TIME HEREFORDS RECORDS—BATTING

Team Batting: .300 in 1950

Games Played: 141 • **Stan Galle**; 1951

At Bats: 612 • **James England**; 1952

Hits: 198 • **James England**; 1952

Doubles: 48 • **Ron Jackson**; 1950

Triples: 18 • **Richard Sobeck**; 1953

Home Runs: 39 • **Steve Molinari**; 1950

Batting Average: .363 • **Walt Massefski**; 1954

Slugging Percentage: .683 • **Steve Molinari**; 1950

Total Bases: 330 • **Steve Molinari**; 1950

Runs Batted In: 162 • **Steve Molinari**; 1950

ALL-TIME HEREFORDS RECORDS—PITCHING

Wins: 26 • **Bill Donaghey**; 1950

Losses: 19 • **James Harper**; 1951

Winning Percentage: .917 • **Bill Starr**; 1950

Earned Ron Average: 2.00 • **Forest Smith**; 1947

Game Appearances: 50 • **Frank Grass**; 1950

Innings Pitched: 265 • **Forest Smith**; 1947

Hits Allowed: 300 • **J. L. Rhodes**; 1954

Bases on Balls: 189 • **James Harper**; 1951

Strike Outs: 267 • **Ted Gardner;** 1949

ALL-TIME HEREFORDS RECORDS—FIELDING

Team Fielding: .938 in 1952 and 1953

Catchers: .985 • **Leonard Zeibig**; 1950

First Base: .988 • **Tony Costa**; 1953

Second Base: .967 • **Bobby King**; 1949

Third Base: .900 • **Ron Slawski**; 1952

Shortstop: .916 • **Jack Ray**; 1950

Outfielders: .984 • **Bob Bonebrake**; 1953

YEAR BY YEAR LEADERS OF EIGHT SEASONS

(*=led league)

The first edition of the Herefords played to the largest crowds of any Ada team, 41,872. Led at bat by Paul Richardville and on the mound by Forest Smith in his last season as a hurler, the Browns' farm hands posted a record of 86-51 10½ games behind champion Lawton, but 14½ games ahead of third-place McAlester. The third and fourth place clubs, McAlester and Ardmore, eliminated Ada and Lawton respectively, in the first playoff round. McAlester filled with future Yankees established its habit of winning the playoffs.

Team Batting: .251 (fifth of six)

Team Fielding: .921 (fifth of six)

Paul Richardville—Games: 137 • At Bats: 530 • Hits:161 • Doubles: 37
 • Home Runs: 11* • Total Bases: 245 • Runs Batted In: 111*

Howard Wooster—Triples: 8

Joe Isaacs—Batting Average: .326 • Slugging Percentage: .528

Forest "Woody" Smith—Wins: 23* • Winning Percentage: .767
 • Earned Run Average: 2.00* • Game Appearances: 39
 • Innings Pitched: 265 • Hits Allowed: 225

Jack Wilson—Losses: 11

Bill Donaghey—Runs Allowed: 124 • Bases on Balls: 137 • Strike Outs: 244*

FIELDING

Catcher: **Robert Kopkea** and **Jack Nesbit** .967

First Base: **Bill Hughes** .969

Second Base: **Howard Wooster** .919

Third Base: **Ray Kolafa** .874

Shortstop: **Robert Boddy** .863

Outfield: **Paul Deters** .943

Once again, two Herefords dominated. Frank Hensley led in all hitting categories but average. Harry Vice was the workhorse on the mound while James Howard led in strike outs but was wild, giving up thirty more walks than "Ks." Nearly 14,000 fewer fans, only 27,050, came out to see Uke Clanton's young Herefords finish fifth in the expanded Sooner State League with a record of 63-76.

Team Batting: .249 (sixth of eight)

Team Fielding: .936 (fourth of eight)

Frank Hensley—Games: 136 • At Bats: .543 • Hits: 155 • Doubles: 29
• Triples: 5 • Home Runs: 15 • Slugging Percentage: .440
• Total Bases: 239 • Runs Batted In: 100

Arnold Spence—Batting Average: .294

Harry Vice—Wins: 15 • Losses: 11 • Winning Percentage: .577
• Game Appearances: 41 • Innings Pitched: 213
• Hits Allowed: 187

Virl Loman—Earned Run Average: 3.72

James Howard—Runs Allowed: 135 • Bases on Balls: 171
• Strike Outs: 149

FIELDING

Catcher: **Charles Hopkins** .966

First Base: **Earl Bossenberry** .980

Second Base: **Bobby King** .946

Third Base: **Wayne Ingram** .916

Shortstop: **Dennis Rackley** .891

Outfield: **Art Spence** .958

The 1949 Herefords, with several returnees from 1948, responded to new ownership and a new manager, Bill Krueger, with a record just under .500, 69-70, but good enough for the playoffs. The team hitting was weak but four players topped the club: Fred Boiko, Les Williams, Bill Milligan, and Earl Bossenberry. Ted Gardner was the workhorse while Ralph Herman posted the best winning percentage and ERA. Attendance was up more than 6,000 from 1948 with 33,525 going through the Hereford Park turnstiles. The Herefords lost to regular season winner Pauls Valley in the first round of the playoff in five games.

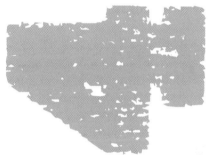

Team Batting: .230 (eighth of eight)

Team Fielding: .945 (fourth of eight)

Fred Boiko—Games: 134 • Home Runs: 9

Lester Williams—At Bats: 549 • Hits: 139 • Doubles: 26
• Runs Batted In: 91 • Total Bases: 184

Earl Bossenberry—Batting Average: . 274 • Slugging Percentage: .372

Bill Milligan (54 games with Seminole)—Hits: 128 • Doubles: 27
• Batting Average .295 • Runs Batted In: 99 • Total Bases: 199
• Slugging Percentage: .520

Jack Ray—Triples: 6

Bill Krueger—Home Runs 9

Ted Gardner—Wins: 13 • Losses: 14 • Game Appearances: 36
• Innings Pitched: 249 • Runs Allowed: 121
• Bases on Balls: 170 • Strike Outs: 267

John Schwartz—Wins 13

Ralph Herman—Winning Percentage: .667 • Earned Run Average: 2.78

Virl Loman—Hits Allowed: 239

FIELDING

Catcher: **Leonard Zeibig** .924

First Base: **Earl Bossenberry** .981

Second Base: **Bobby King** .967

Third Base: **Bill Krueger** .894

Shortstop: **Henry Pengel** .874

Outfield: **Fred Boiko** .974

The best club St. Louis sent was made up of returnees from 1949 and 1947 alumnus Bill Donaghey who posted 26 wins. Krueger's second team coasted to a regular season championship with a record of 96-41, 5½ games ahead of second place McAlester. Steve Molinari was the story at the plate as he set the Sooner State League record for home runs. Once again, the Herefords could not get past the first playoff round, this time losing to independent Ardmore in five. Despite the best play ever in Ada, attendance dropped off to 31,981.

Team Batting: .300 (first of eight)

Team Fielding: .931 (fifth of eight)

Fred Boiko—Games: 138 • At Bats: 578 • Hits: 190

Ron Jackson—Doubles: 48 • Triples: 6

Bill Milligan—Triples 6

Steve Molinari—Home Runs: 39* • Slugging Percentage: .683
• Total Bases: 330 • Runs Batted In: 162*

Bill Krueger—Batting Average: .349

Bill Donaghey—Wins: 26 • Innings Pitched: 265 • Hits Allowed: 262
• Strike Outs: 199

Ted Szymanski—Losses: 11 • Runs Allowed: 166 • Bases on Balls: 142

William Starr—Winning Percentage: .917

Frank Grass—Earned Run Average: 3.65
• Game Appearances: 50 • Strike Outs: 199

FIELDING

Catcher: **Leonard Zeibig** .985

First Base: **Don Davenport** .980

Second Base: **Ron Jackson** .932

Third Base: **Bill Krueger** .888

Shortstop: **Jack Ray** .898

Outfield: **Fred Boiko** .963

Manager Stan Galle led in most batting categories while Richard Sobeck provided the long ball but to no avail as the 1951 version of the Herefords dropped to fifth place with a .368 percentage in a badly balanced league. The worst attendance in Ada history, and second worst in Sooner State League history, only 12,779 witnessed the 54-86 season. Owner Bob Cason fire-sold the team to a new investor group.

Team Batting: .248 (sixth of eight)

Team Fielding: .930 (sixth of eight)

Stan Galle—Games: 141 • At Bats: 552 • Hits: 175 • Doubles: 30
　　• Batting Average: .317 • Runs Batted In: 112

Richard Sobeck—Games 141 • Triples: 13 • Home Runs: 19
　　• Total Bases: 276

Joe Carolan—Slugging Percentage: .550

William Diemer—Wins: 15 • Winning Percentage: .517

James Harper—Losses: 19 • Hits Allowed: 259 • Runs Allowed: 226
　　• Bases on Balls: 189 • Strike Outs: 217

Richard Glockzin—Earned Run Average: 4.55

Jerry Kroger—Game Appearances: 44 • Innings Pitched: 227

FIELDING

Catcher: **Arnold Jesse** .953

First Base: **Elmer Haslip** .979

Second Base: **Stan Galle** .952

Third Base: **Merle Barth** .840

Shortstop: **Jack Ray** .916

Outfield: **Richard Sobeck** .977

Attendance tripled from 1951 to 38,387 under new owner-ship to watch the worst club Ada ever fielded finish seventh with a 57-82 record. Back for a second season, Richard Sobeck was the best hitter while Neil Thode pulled the laboring oar for the pitching staff.

Team Batting: .273 (third of eight)

Team Fielding: .938 (fifth of eight)

Robert Barron—Games: 140 • Doubles: 31

James England—Games: 140 • At Bats: 612* • Hits: 198*

Richard Sobeck—Triples: 18 • Home Runs: 19
- Batting Average: .347 • Slugging Percentage: .577
- Total Bases: 299 • Runs Batted In: 127

Neil Thode—Wins: 13 • Losses: 18 • Game Appearances: 29
- Innings Pitched: 246 • Hits Allowed: 269
- Runs Allowed: 175 • Bases on Balls: 162 • Strike Outs: 193

Harold Byfuss—Winning Percentage: .615

Earl Gunner—Earned Run Average: 2.95

FIELDING

Catcher: **Mike Goffredo** .963

First Base: **Bill Enos** .980

Second Base: **James England** .946

Third Base: **Ron Slawski** .900

Shortstop: **Robert Barron** .901

Outfield: **Richard Sobeck** .961

A much better and more balanced ball club, plus the pitching heroics of rookie J. L. Rhodes, brought 36,128 Pontotoc County fans out to the ball park to see Lou Brower's 84-54 Herefords finish third 7½ games behind first place Ardmore then beat Shawnee in four games to face nemesis McAlester in Ada's first and only appearance in the playoff finals. The McAlester jinx held with the Herefords losing in five games.

Team Batting: .270 (first of eight)

Team Fielding: .938 (sixth of eight)

Don McGregor—Games: 137 Triples: 7

Ron Slawski—At Bats: 551 • Home Runs 31* • Total Bases: 274
   • Runs Batted In: 109

Tony Costa—Hits: 175

George Blash—Doubles: 41

Robert Norden—Home Runs: 31*

Bob Bonebrake—Batting Average: .353
   • Slugging Percentage: .577

J. L. Rhodes—Wins: 21* • Winning Percentage: .778
   • Earned Run Average: 3.20 • Game Appearances: 33
   • Innings Pitched: 228 • Hits Allowed: 218 • Strike Outs: 192

George Werrmann—Losses: 10

Ron Coburn—Losses 10 • Runs Allowed: 130 • Bases on Balls: 136

FIELDING

Catcher: **Mike Goffredo** .980

First Base: **Tony Costa** .988

Second Base: **Chico Gonzales** .936

Third Base: **Ron Slawski** .857

Shortstop: **Don McGregor** .893

Outfield: **Bob Bonebrake** .984

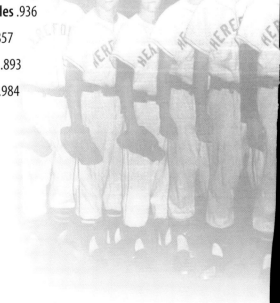

Weather, poor attendance, and the insolvency of the Ada Baseball Association plagued the last edition of the Herefords. Walt Massefski, picked up on the bounce from the Cubs' farm club at Gainesville, tore up league pitching. Richard Lubinski added the long ball. Latecomer Fern Smathers went on a hitting rampage before settling in for a .323 performance. J. L. Rhodes continued his fine pitching but the rest of the club provided little help. Attendance fell to 28,482 for the sixth place Ada nine that finished with a 64-76 record. The new owner was unable to secure a working agreement and the Ada franchise moved south to Paris, Texas.

Team Batting: .272 (fourth of eight)
Team Fielding: .932 (eighth of eight)

Ron Barbian—Games: 139 • At Bats: 520 • Doubles: 32
Walt Massefski—Hits: 182 • Batting Average: .363
    • Slugging Percentage: .550 • Triples: 8 • Total Bases: 276
Richard Lubinski—Home Runs: 28 • Runs Batted In: 115
J. L. Rhodes—Wins: 18 • Winning Percentage: .581
    • Earned Run Average: 3.83 • Game Appearances: 39
    • Innings Pitched: 261 • Hits Allowed: 300 • Runs Allowed: 180
    • Strike Outs: 190
Ruben Saager—Losses: 15 • Bases on Balls: 135

FIELDING

Catcher: **Fern Smathers** .977
First Base: **Ron Barbian** .973
Second Base: **James Samford** .967
Third Base: **John Densmore** .866
Shortstop: **Ken Hinton** .875
Outfield: **Bruce Lane** .920

BIBLIOGRAPHY

Burke, Bob, Franks, Kenny, Parr, Royse, *Glory Days of Summer: The History of Baseball in Oklahoma*, Oklahoma City: Oklahoma Heritage Association 1999.

Johnson, Lloyd and Miles Wolff ed., *The Encyclopedia of Minor League Baseball*, 3d ed. Durham, NC: Baseball America, Inc. 2007

Pierce, Peter G., *Baseball in the Cross Timbers: The Story of the Sooner State League*, Oklahoma City: Oklahoma Heritage Association 2009

—*Indians, Cardinals & Rosebuds: Professional Baseball in Ardmore 1947-1961* Oklahoma City: Oklahoma Heritage Association 2011

Society for American Baseball Research, *SABR Minor Leagues Database*, http://www.baseball-reference.com/minors

Spink, J. G. Taylor, *Official Baseball Guide and Record Book*, St.Louis: Charles C. Spink & Son 1946-1955 inclusive

PERIODICALS

Ada Evening News 1946-1955

The Daily Ardmoreite 1946-1955

The Daily Oklahoman 1946-1955

The Sporting News 1946-1955

INTERVIEWS

Bill Thrash, bat boy Ada Herefords 1952-1953, several between 2008 and 2011, at Oklahoma City

Bobby King, second baseman Ada Herefords 1948-1949, several 2011, telephone

Charles Hopkins, catcher Ada Herefords 1948, December 3, 2011, telephone

Fern Smathers, catcher Ada Herefords/Cementers, July 2008, Baton Rouge, LA

PHOTOS AND CREDITS

Front cover: Bobby King (hereafter "King")

8 (left) Derril McGuire

8 (center) King

8 (right) Charles Hopkins (hereafter "Hopkins)

9 (left) John Hall

9 (center) Stephens County Historical Museum, Duncan, Oklahoma

9 (right) Author's Collection

10 (left) *Ada Evening News* April, 1947

10 (upper right) Van Yount (hereafter "Yount")

10 (lower right) King

11 (upper left) Harry Stevens www.net54baseball.com

11 (right) Durham Convention and Visitors' Bureau

11 (lower left) Hopkins

12 (upper left) *Chickasha Express*

12 (upper right) Mrs. Tom Kruta

12 (middle right) Yount

12 (lower right) King

12 (lower left) Obituary, *Toledo Blade*, September 22, 2011

13 (all) King

14 (upper left) Hopkins

14 (upper right) Bill Thrash (hereafter "Thrash")

14 (middle left) Yount

14 (lower left) Hopkins

15 (upper) Roger Willingham

15 (lower) Yount

16 (all) King

17 (all) King

18 (upper) Ann Milligan

18 (lower) King

19 (upper right) 35th Infantry Regiment Association

19 (lower left) Author's Collection

20 Oklahoma Heritage Association from *Indians, Cardinals & Rosebuds*

21-28 Thrash

29 Thrash

31 (all) Thrash

32 (all) Thrash

33 (upper) Thrash

33 (lower) *The Paris News*

34 (all) Thrash

35 (upper left) Thrash

35 (upper right) Jay Publishing

35 (lower right) *The Paris News*

36 Thrash

37 Fern Smathers

39 (upper)*Ada Evening News* August, 1938

39 (middle right) Author's Collection

39 (middle left and lower) Hopkins

40 (all) King

42 (upper left) www.en.wikipedia.org

42 (lower right) Thrash

43 Opal Cole Canada

44 (upper right) Mobile Sports Hall of Fame

44 (lower left) King

44 (lower middle) John Hall

44 (lower right) Cape Cod Hall of Fame www.capecodbaseball.org

45 (upper) King

45 (lower) Thrash

46 (upper left, lower right) Author's Collection

46 www.sonsofsamhorn.com

47 King

48 Fern and Joanna Smathers

49 (upper) King

49 (lower) Thrash

Back cover: (left) Hopkins (right) Laurie Anne Williams

INDEX